THE OFFICIAL WORKBOOK
MINECRAFT
GRADE 2

Written by Russell Ginns
Illustrations by Antonio Vecchione

WELCOME TO A LEARNING ADVENTURE!

This workbook lets kids practice essential skills while taking a journey through the world of Minecraft. Learn to count while exploring a cave and practice vocabulary while crafting armor! There are dozens of activities filled with reading, math, and critical-thinking skills, all set among the biomes, mobs, and loot of your child's favorite game.

Special Minecraft Missions at the end of each lesson also send readers on learning challenges inside and outside the book!

Here are some tips to make the most of this workbook:

- Make sure your child has a quiet, comfortable place to work.

- Give your child a variety of pencils, crayons, and any other items they may need to write answers, draw pictures, or set up games.

- Read the directions with your child. There's a lot of information and adventures packed into each chapter! You can help tell the stories and point out the basic tasks that need to be done.

- Spend extra time on any section that your child finds difficult.

- Enjoy the fun Minecraft facts and jokes with your child. This is your chance to learn more about a game that interests them!

**Grab a pen or pencil and get ready to
have fun as you learn with Minecraft!**

SEARCH THE SANDS

You've arrived in the desert. There are things to discover, collect... and avoid!

In this adventure, you will...

Collect sticks.

Search the dunes.

Craft a shovel.

Uncover a buried temple.

Let's get started!

+10

The desert may be mostly sand, but sooner or later you'll likely stumble on some dead bushes as you explore. When you do, break them to collect sticks!

There are seven **sight words** in the **shrubs** (❦) below. Circle all the **sticks** (✎) with matching sight words that are spelled correctly.

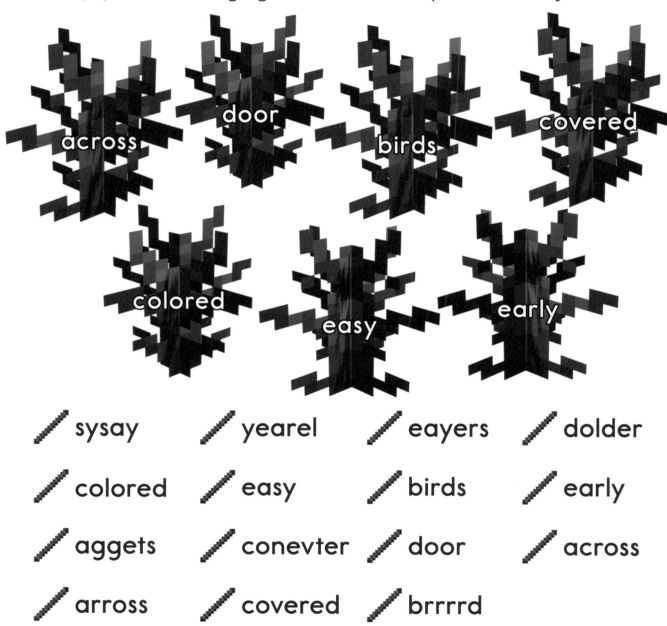

across   door   birds   covered

colored   easy   early

✎ sysay	✎ yearel	✎ eayers	✎ dolder
✎ colored	✎ easy	✎ birds	✎ early
✎ aggets	✎ conevter	✎ door	✎ across
✎ arross	✎ covered	✎ brrrrd	

MINECRAFT FACT: Without trees in the desert, breaking dead shrubs is the easiest way to collect sticks.

Draw a line to connect pairs of sticks to form words. Then write each full word in the space to the right.

fr	rm	____________
fi	ld	____________
fa	sh	____________
fie	iend	____________
hap	ound	____________
gr	pen	____________
k	red	____________
hund	ing	____________
lis	ten	____________

You did it! Place your sticker here.

Explore the desert. There's something hidden out there, forgotten by time.

Find a path from **START** to **END**. You may only pass through words from the list below.

Find these words:

short	today	knew	music	question
reach	south	usual	low	problem

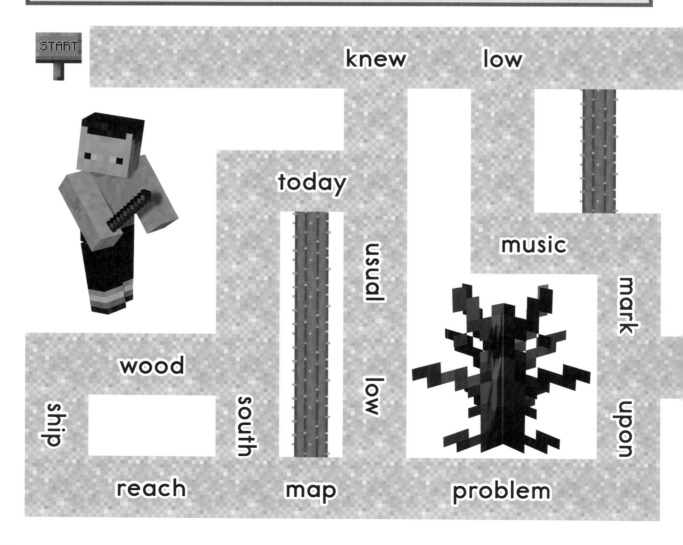

START

knew · low

today

usual

music

mark

wood

south · low

ship

reach · map · problem

upon

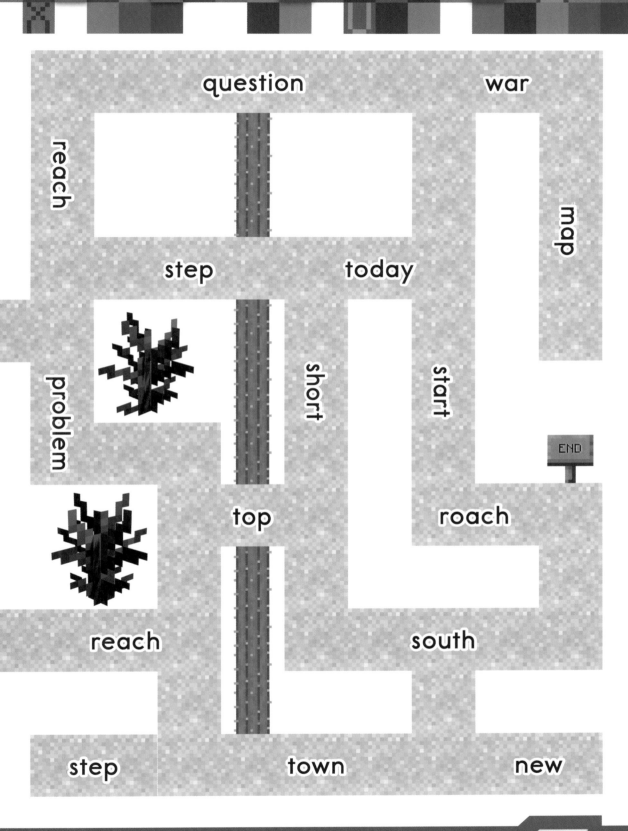

question

war

reach

map

step

today

problem

short

start

END

top

roach

reach

south

step

town

new

Use wood to craft a shovel so you can uncover this sandy mystery.

Cross out one letter from each crafting table so that each group forms a real **silent e** word.

Circle the four words you just spelled.

where	horse	piece	since
place	sure	table	wave

Complete the **silent e** words next to each shovel by filling in the missing letters.

🔨 __rue

🔨 becom__

🔨 co__plete

🔨 s__ace

🔨 samp__e

🔨 insid__

Write the letters you used in the spaces below. They will spell what you've discovered!

__ __ __ __ __ __

You unearthed a desert temple with a secret room! Be very careful as you search the temple for loot.

Unscramble the letters and write the correct words in the spaces.

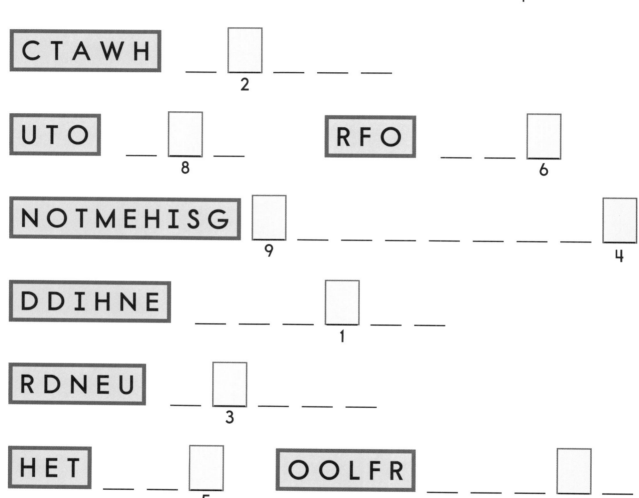

CTAWH   __ ☐ __ __ __
         2

UTO   __ ☐ __   RFO   __ __ ☐
       8   6

NOTMEHISG   ☐ __ __ __ __ __ __ __ ☐
             9   4

DDIHNE   __ __ __ ☐ __ __
                   1

RDNEU   __ ☐ __ __ __
          3

HET   __ __ ☐   OOLFR   __ __ __ ☐ __
             5   7

Write the letters from each shaded space above into the space below with the matching number. You'll spell one more important word.

__ __ __ __ __ __ __ __ __
1 2 3 4 5 6 7 8 9

Why did the adventurer pack a spoon instead of a shovel?
He thought he was going to a dessert.

Complete each word to avoid triggering the temple's traps. When you're done, the words will tell you what you've discovered.

Use these letters:

st r nd ha o

it lle es asu

Y_u ju__

fou__ ch__ts

t__t a_e

fi___d w__h

tre___re!

MINECRAFT MISSION

You explored a desert and found treasure. Now explore your world with a special challenge.

This mission sends you *outside* of this book! Your task is to explore the different regions of your home and search for things that fit these rules:

- Find something that contains the letter **x**
- Find something that ends with the letter **y**
- Find something that contains the letter **z**
- Find five things with names that contain *two letters of the alphabet in a row* (for example, **de**, **hi**, **lm**, or **st**)

Write the items you find on the lines below, and have an adult check your work. Then find the correct sticker and place it in the lower corner. You've completed your first mission!

_____   _____

_____   _____

_____   _____

_____   _____

MINECRAFT

DISCOVER

Great job! You earned a badge! Place your sticker here.

GROW

SETTLE DOWN

With a farm, you can plant and harvest many crops.

In this adventure, you will...

Collect seeds.

Craft a hoe.

Plant crops.

Water plants.

Let's get started!

Search the tall grass to find wheat seeds. Other crops can also grow from different kinds of seeds, like pumpkin, melon, and beetroot.

Add to solve each problem.

2 + 6 = _____

5 + 6 = _____

3 + 7 = _____

4 + 12 = _____

8 + 10 = _____

2 + 13 = _____

Copy your answers above into the rows below so the amount in each group of seeds goes from **smallest** to **largest**.

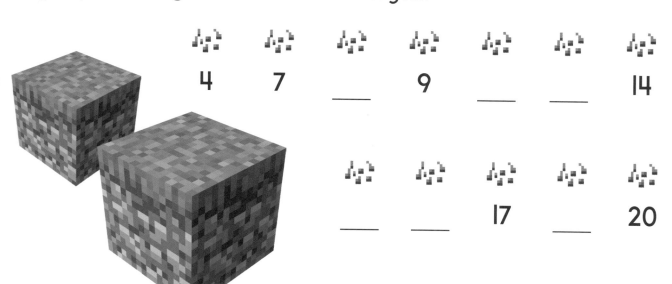

4   7   ___   9   ___   ___   14

___   ___   17   ___   20

MINECRAFT FACT: One way to collect seeds is to interact with a sniffer, a passive mob that sniffs out and digs for seeds.

Fill in the blanks below so the plant problems are correctly solved.

13 + _____ = 19

4 + _____ = 9

8 + _____ = 20

_____ + 8 = 15

_____ + 11 = 20

9 + _____ = 10

14 + _____ = 19

_____ + 10 = 29

20 + _____ = 30

_____ + 15 = 25

If you have a hoe, you can farm in style.
Craft some hoes using sticks and stones.

Count the items in each group and write the
numbers. Then **subtract** to solve each problem.

 **-**  **=** _____

_____

 **-**  **=** _____

_____

 **-**  **=** _____

_____

*MINECRAFT FACT: A hoe is the only tool that can be used to turn
normal dirt into farmland—the perfect place to plant your crops.*

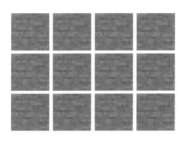 -  = _____

_____   _____

 -  = _____

_____   _____

 -  = _____

_____   _____

ADDITION AND SUBTRACTION

With your hoe, you've tilled the ground and created a great place to plant a sugar cane crop.

Draw more sugar cane so that the total number is equal to the number shown. The first one has been done for you.

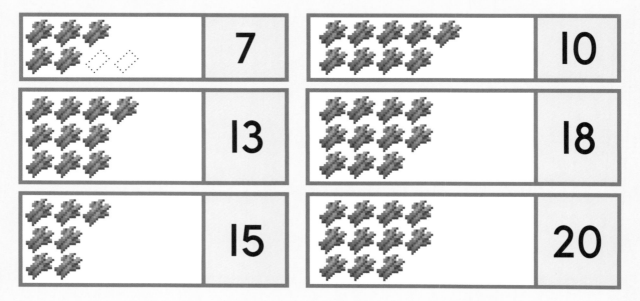

Cross out sugar cane below so that the value of the leftover sugar cane matches the number shown.

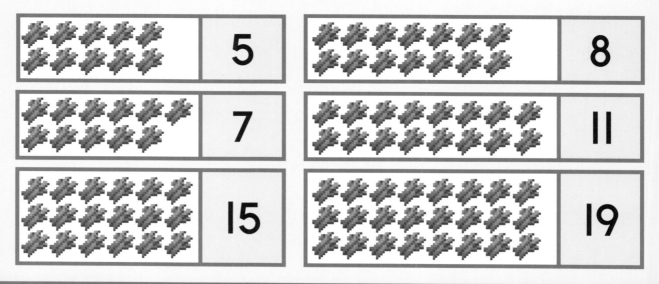

MINECRAFT FACT: As long as your farmland is within four blocks of a water source, crops will stay hydrated.

Circle all the problems that are correct.

W $14 + 5 = 19$ H $12 + 9 = 20$

A $11 - 10 = 1$ O $15 - 11 = 7$

F $30 - 15 = 5$ T $15 + 5 = 20$

E $3 + 19 = 22$ R $20 - 8 = 12$

U $16 - 9 = 7$ S $24 + 6 = 30$

G $21 + 8 = 27$ Y $16 + 19 = 30$

Now copy the letters from all the circled problems into the spaces below, starting from the top and moving left to right. They'll spell an important message from the plants!

___ ___ ___ ___ ___ ___ ___ ___

Keep the ground watered. Then your plants will thrive.

Count your crops by drawing rectangles around **groups of ten** plants.

How many groups of ten did you make? _____

Why did Santa Claus build a farm in Minecraft? To hoe, hoe, hoe!

20

Count the number of plants in each **hundreds**, **tens**, and **ones** stack. Then write the number below and read the full value aloud.

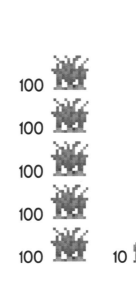

1

1

10   1

10   1

100   10   1

100   10   1

100

100

100

100

100   10   1

___   ___   ___   ___   ___   ___

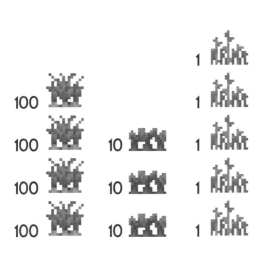

1

100   1

100   10   1

100   10   1

100   10   1

10   1

10   1

10   1

10   1

100   10   1

___   ___   ___   ___   ___   ___

MINECRAFT MISSION

Your farm is up and running. Now take this challenge and learn what you've accomplished.

Solve this mission by searching for these **crops** ( ) hidden in the top sections of this book!

Write the page number where you find each item in the matching space below. The first one has been done for you.

20 ____ ____ ____ ____ ____ ____

Now look at the numbers below. Circle any that match the page numbers you found, then copy the letters above each into the spaces below. This will reveal what you've gained with your hard work!

H	G	B	A	R	L	C
56	14	64	50	26	43	82

V	P	J	E	N	S	T
22	75	39	20	57	89	35

____ ____ ____ ____ ____ ____ ____

MINECRAFT GROW

Great job! You earned a badge! Place your sticker here.

TUNNEL VISION

You've reached the mountains—filled with caves, ore, and more!

In this adventure, you will...

Explore mountains.

Enter a cave.

Light up the darkness.

Cross a lava pool.

Let's get started!

Head up to the mountains, where you can find caves—
and maybe treasure.

Follow each trail up into the mountains and read the letters you pass
along the way. Then write three words that end in that **letter blend**.
The first one has been done for you.

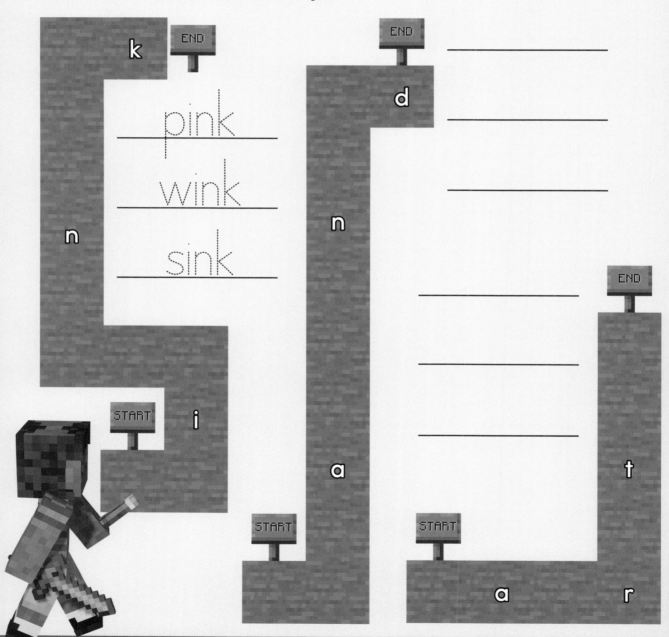

MINECRAFT FACT: Caves often contain water or lava flows.

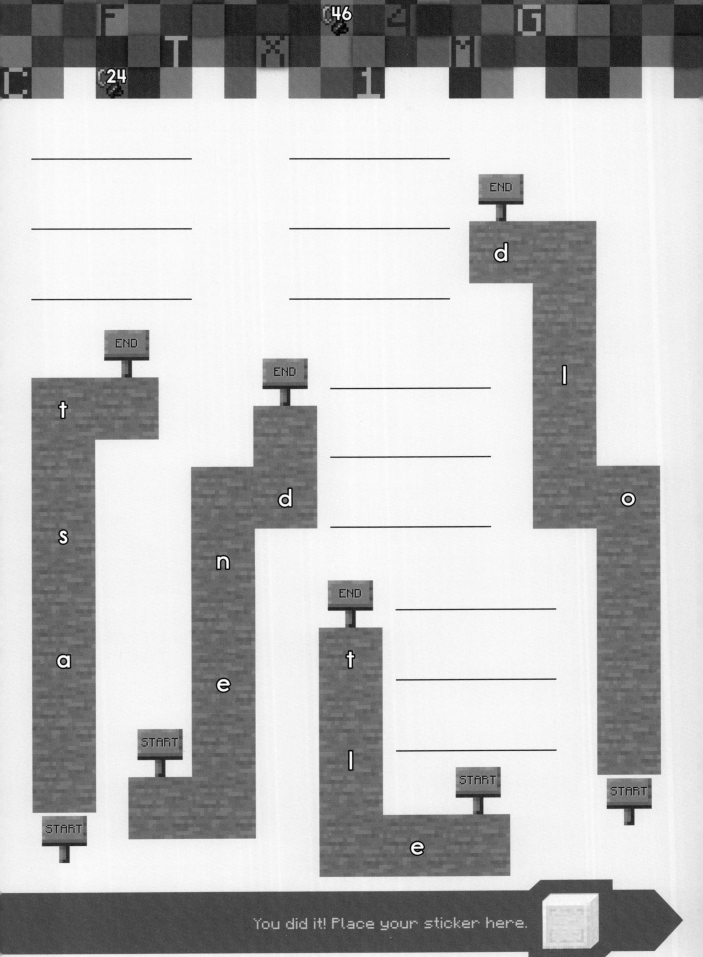

You did it! Place your sticker here.

DOUBLE LETTERS

D

You found a cave! Head inside, deep into uncharted territory.

Find a safe path through this cave from **START** to **END** that only passes through words that end with **double letters** (two of the same letter).

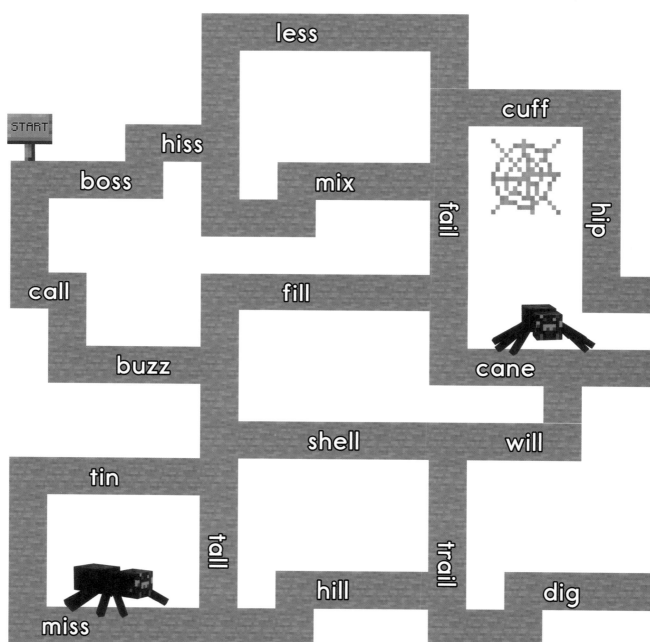

less

cuff

START

hiss

boss

mix

fail

hip

call

fill

buzz

cane

shell

will

tin

tall

trail

hill

dig

miss

MINECRAFT FACT: Deeper caves are often filled with a strong, dark stone called deepslate.

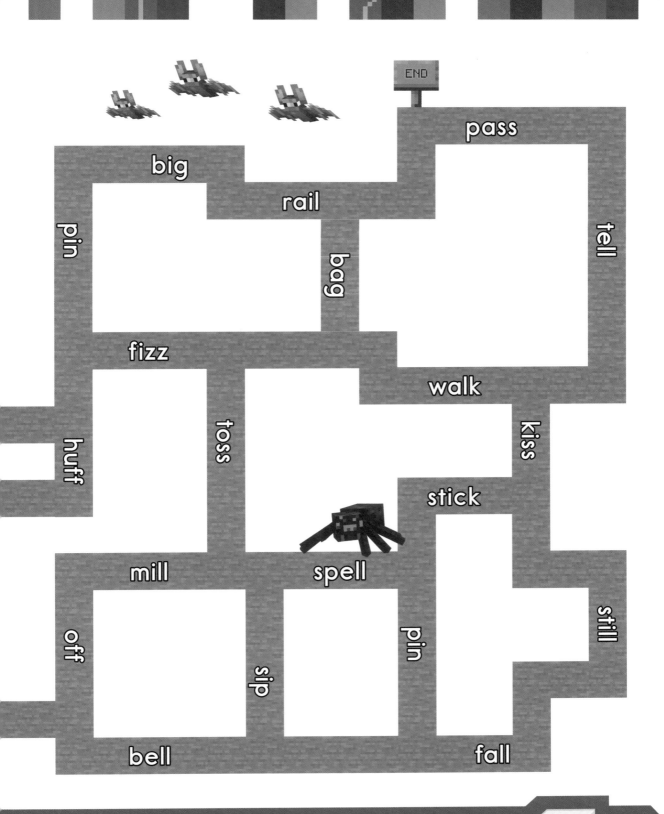

big

pass

pin

rail

tell

bag

fizz

walk

huff

toss

kiss

stick

mill

spell

still

off

sip

pin

fall

bell

You did it! Place your sticker here.

Leave a trail of torches to find your way through the darkness.

Complete the **double-vowel** words below using the torches in the letter bank. Each torch can only be used once.

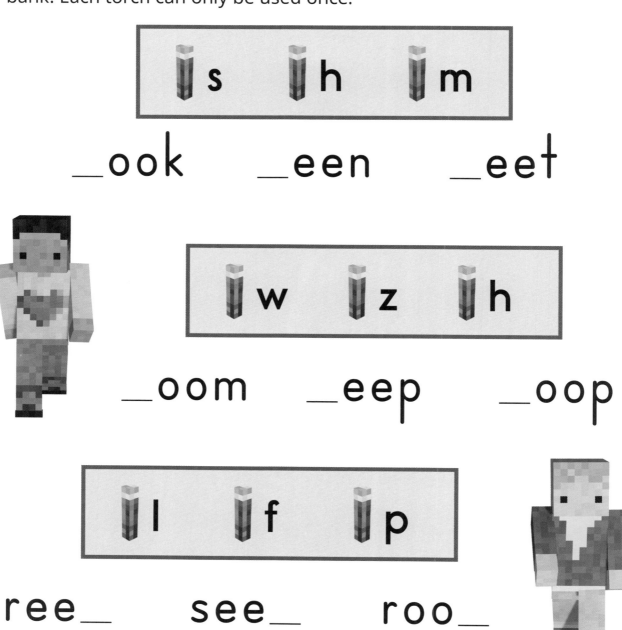

s   h   m

__ook   __een   __eet

w   z   h

__oom   __eep   __oop

l   f   p

ree__   see__   roo__

MINECRAFT FACT: In a cave, torches prevent hostile mobs from spawning and help you find your way out.

Complete the double-vowel words below using the torches in the letter bank. Each torch can be used more than once.

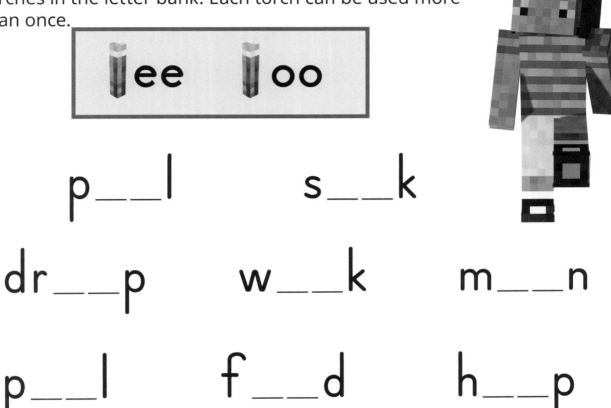

ee   oo

p__l   s__k

dr__p   w__k   m__n

p__l   f__d   h__p

Pick one torch that can be used to complete *all* the words below.

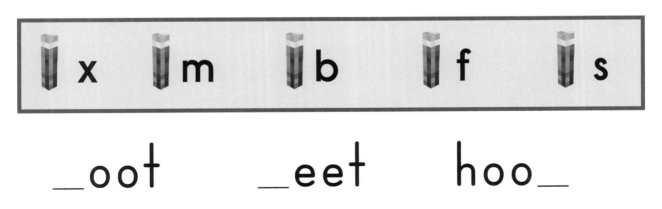

x   m   b   f   s

_oot   _eet   hoo_

You reached a field of lava pools. Build bridges to reach the other side.

Use the **letter blends** bank on page 31 to fill in the missing letters to complete each word. Each letter blend will only be used once.

F O ▢ ▢

W I ▢ ▢   B E ▢ ▢

▢ ▢ A G

▢ ▢ O R T

L E ▢ ▢

What kind of music do stone blocks like? *Rock and roll.*

Use these letters:

GR RT BL SH BR

SP ND CT NS

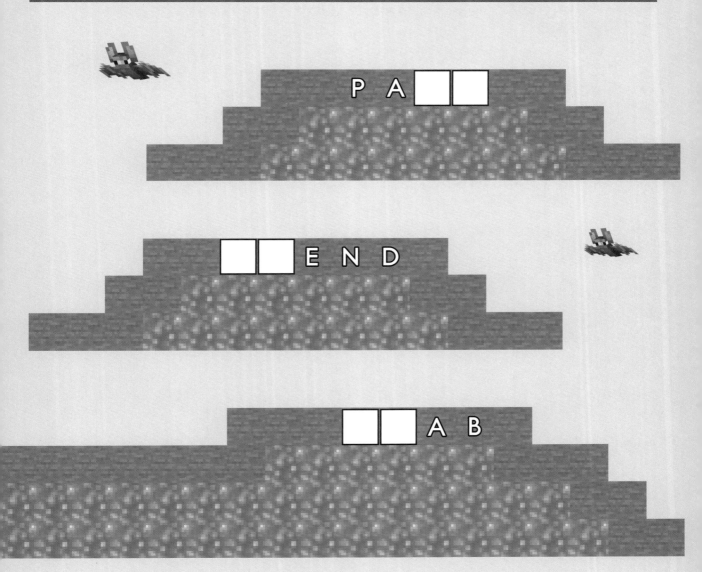

P A ☐ ☐

☐ ☐ E N D

☐ ☐ A B

You did it! Place your sticker here.

MINECRAFT MISSION

You've made it across the lava! Now travel outside this book for a new challenge.

This mission sends you *outside* of this book! Decorate your room with signs and posters you'll make while using some of the words from this adventure.

You'll need:

- Crayons
- Paper
- Pencils
- Scissors
- Tape

Make these things:

- A sign to hang on your door
- Three different labels to put on things you own
- A movie-style poster about something that happens during a Minecraft adventure

Here's the challenge:

- Everything you make must feature at least one word with a two-consonant letter blend

Example words:

wo**rk**	**sl**eep	**st**op
show	**cr**a**ft**	**pl**ay

MINECRAFT

EXPLORE

Great job! You earned a badge! Place your sticker here.

MINE, MINE, MINE!

It's time to head deeper into the cave. Who knows what awaits you?

In this adventure, you will...

Navigate a mineshaft.

Slice through cobwebs.

Fight skeletons.

Make an iron pickaxe.

Let's get started!

Mineshafts are tricky. Proceed with caution as you descend underground.

Find a safe path from **START** to **END** that only passes through **odd** numbers.

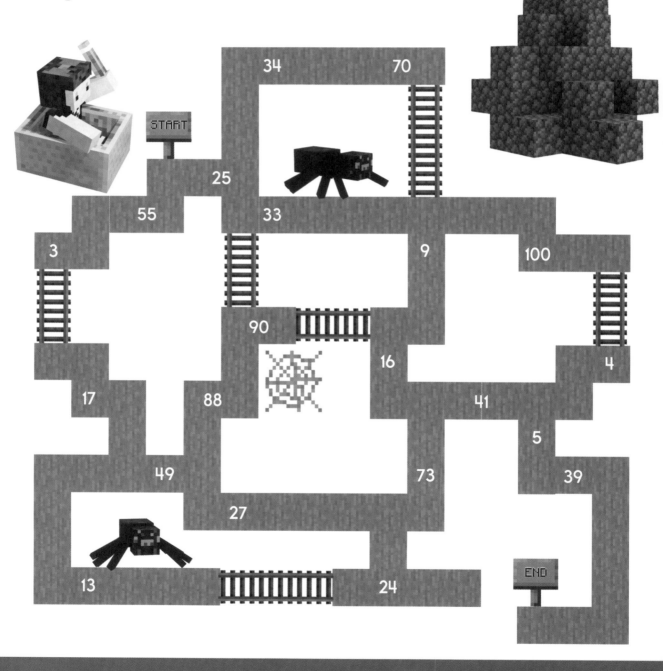

MINECRAFT FACT: Mineshafts can be a great source for ores like gold and iron.

Find a safe path from **START** to **END** that only passes through **even** numbers.

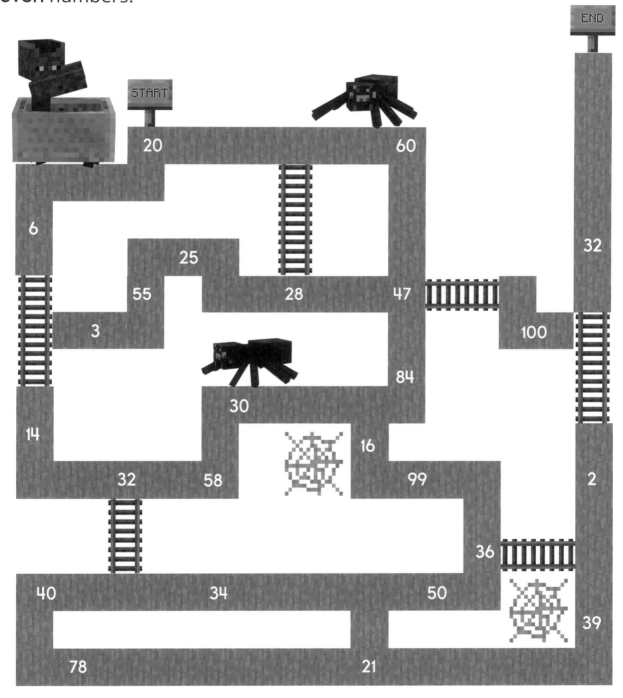

START

END

20   60   32

6

25

55   28   47   100

3

84

30

14   16

32   58   99   2

36

40   34   50   39

78   21

There are cobwebs everywhere. Use your sword to slice them so you can move forward.

Count by **tens** and slice every **tenth** cobweb.

1	2	3	4	5	6	7	8
9	10	11	12	13	14	15	16
17	18	19	20	21	22	23	24
25	26	27	28	29	30	31	32
33	34	35	36	37	38	39	40
41	42	43	44	45	46	47	48
49	50	51	52	53	54	55	56
57	58	59	60	61	62	63	64
		65	66	67	68	69	70

MINECRAFT FACT: Cobwebs slow you down but can be cut quickly with a sword or shears.

Counting by **hundreds**, fill in the missing numbers to help each player reach the end of each mineshaft.

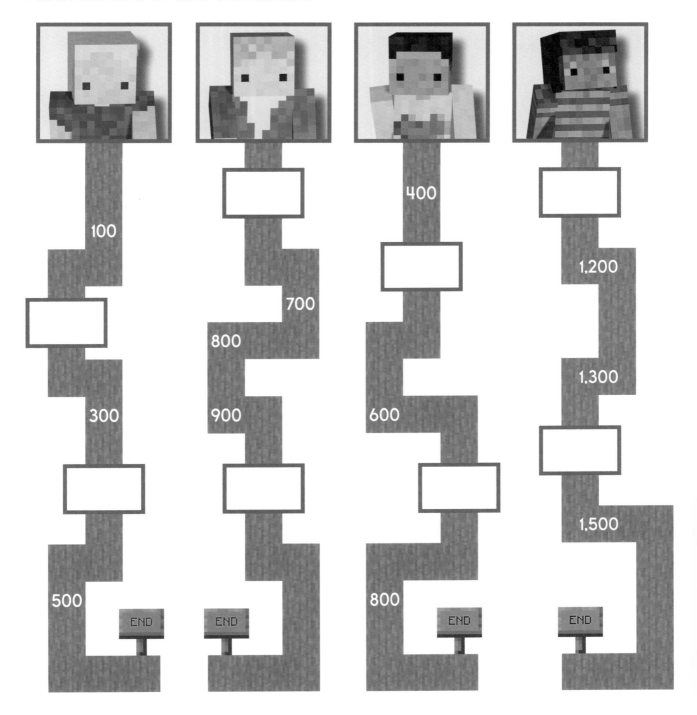

Player 1: 100, [ ], 300, [ ], 500

Player 2: [ ], 700, 800, 900, [ ]

Player 3: 400, [ ], 600, [ ], 800

Player 4: [ ], 1,200, 1,300, [ ], 1,500

An arrow whizzes by you! Skeletons are on your trail.

Connect the dots, counting by **fives**...and watch out!

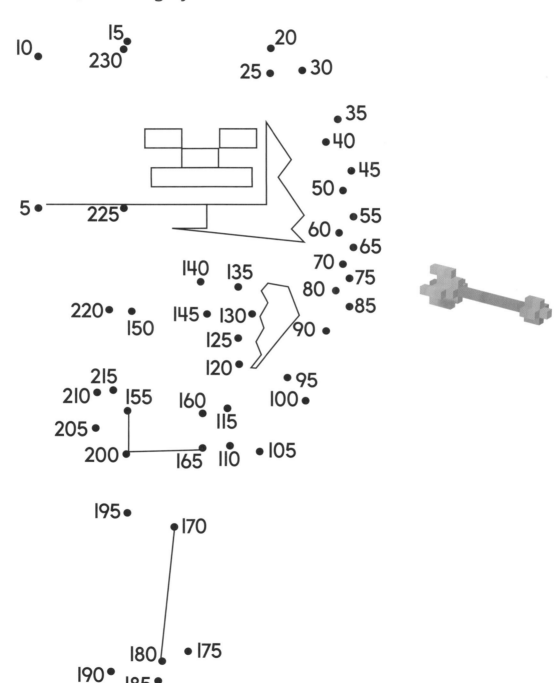

10
15
230
20
25
30
35
40
45
5
225
50
55
60
65
70
75
140
135
80
85
220
150
145
130
90
125
120
215
210
155
160
95
100
205
115
200
165
110
105
195
170
180
175
190
185

Fill in the missing numbers to count by **twenty-fives**.

1	2	3	4	5	6	7	8	9	10

11	12	13	14	15	16	17	18	19	20

21	22	23	24		26	27	28	29	30

31	32	33	34	35	36	37	38	39	40

41	42	43	44	45	46	47	48	49		51	52

53	54	55	56	57	58	59	60	61	62	63	64

65	66	67	68	69	70	71	72	73	74		76

77	78	79	80	81	82	83	84	85	86	87	88

	89	90	91	92	93	94	95	96	97	98

99		101	102	103	104	105	106	107

108	109	110	111	112	113	114	115	116

117	118	119	120	121	122	123	124	

You've found a diamond vein. Use an iron pickaxe to harvest diamond ore.

Write **less than (<)**, **greater than (>)**, or **equal to (=)** in the spaces below to make each statement correct.

7 ⛏ - 1 ⛏ ☐ 4 💎

3 ⛏ + 11 ⛏ ☐ 13 💎

1 ⛏ + 5 ⛏ ☐ 6 💎

10 ⛏ + 10 ⛏ ☐ 16 💎   9 ⛏ + 9 ⛏ ☐ 18 💎

13 ⛏ - 9 ⛏ ☐ 3 💎   6 ⛏ + 8 ⛏ ☐ 12 💎

20 ⛏ - 18 ⛏ ☐ 4 💎   12 ⛏ - 6 ⛏ ☐ 6 💎

16 ⛏ + 3 ⛏ ☐ 20 💎   10 ⛏ + 4 ⛏ ☐ 15 💎

Why did the cave spider get a computer? It was looking for WEB-sites.

Cross out one diamond from each set below, so the total number is the same on both sides.

How many diamonds are on each side? _____

How many diamonds are on each side? _____

How many diamonds are on each side? _____

How many diamonds are on each side? _____

There are so many diamonds to collect! Keep going to find them in this challenge.

This mission sends you on a search *inside* this book. There are items hidden in the top borders of most pages!

Search for pages that have **diamonds** (⬦) at the top. But wait! You can only mine a diamond if it is on an **odd-numbered** page.

Circle the seven diamonds below that match the page numbers of the diamonds you were able to mine. Copy the letters above each one into the spaces at the bottom of the page.

J	B	A	P	M	A	S
27	4	11	37	72	52	16

I	K	C	E	K	F	P
15	19	81	28	69	41	71

O	H	O	Y	D	T	C
45	66	48	9	77	39	58

___ ___ ___ ___ ___ ___ ___

MINECRAFT
SEARCH

Great job! You earned a badge! Place your sticker here.

POWERFUL STUFF

You brought your diamonds home and used them to make an enchanting table. Now get to work!

In this adventure, you will...

Make books.

Fill bookshelves.

Build an enchanting room.

Enchant armor and weapons.

Let's get started!

Craft books from paper and leather to grow your library.

Make nine new **compound words** on page 45. You can use any of the words on this page, or you can think of your own. Write the words, then draw a picture of each one. The first one has been done for you.

 basket   light   air   butter   sun   web

 plain   sea   bulb   pan   sword   back

 fly   cake   house   ball   fish   pack

flash   shine   robe   bath   spider   glasses

 snow   rattle   pit   fall   shoe   snake

MINECRAFT FACT: Villages are spread throughout the world and are home to helpful villagers.

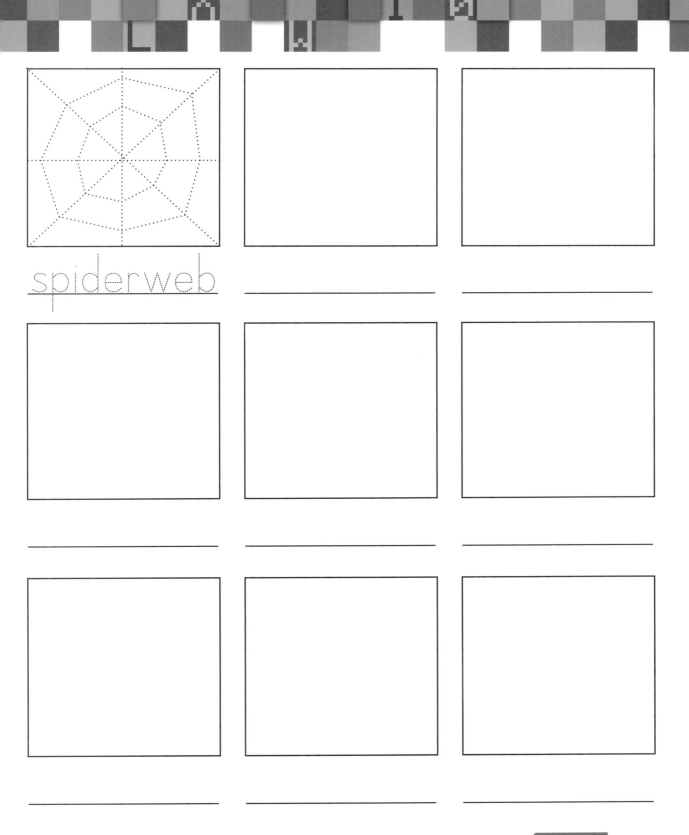

spiderweb

Load up the shelves with your new books.

Arrange the books below so that all the books on a shelf **rhyme**.

Choose from these words:

lit	best	quit	dine
pave	wave	line	test

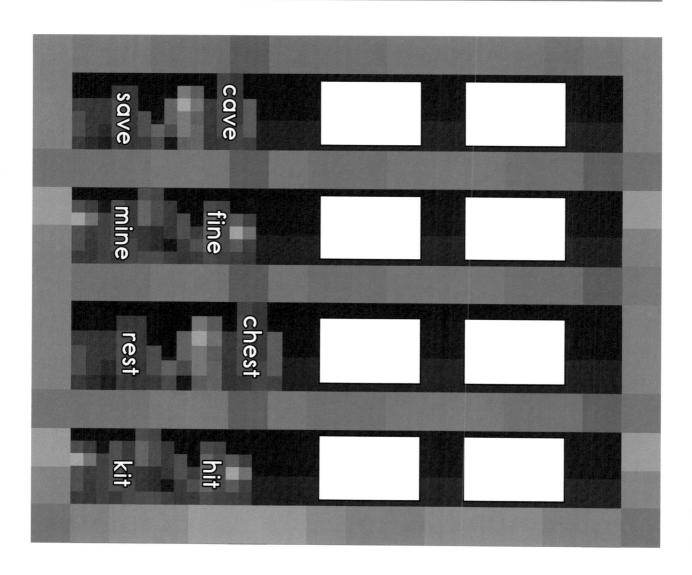

cave   save

fine   mine

chest   rest

kit   hit

MINECRAFT FACT: Chests in villages can hold good loot and helpful items.

Read the word under each book and quill. Then write three words that **rhyme**. The first one has been done for you.

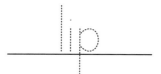

zip   lip   sip   drip

mob _____ _____ _____

red _____ _____ _____

big _____ _____ _____

ten _____ _____ _____

fish _____ _____ _____

run _____ _____ _____

Build the perfect enchanting room to work your magic.

Draw an **oval** around every word that rhymes with **bees**.

Draw a **rectangle** around every word that rhymes with **dark**.

Draw a **star** around every word that rhymes with **catch**.

patch

biome

attack

fish

seas

house

park

gold

dig

latch

pickaxe

cheese

cow

please

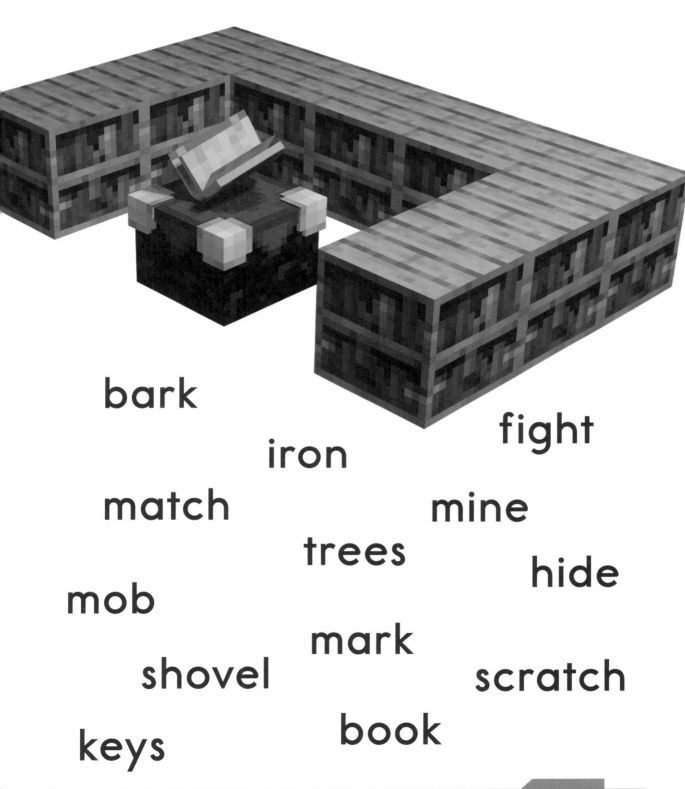

bark

iron

fight

match

mine

trees

hide

mob

mark

shovel

scratch

keys

book

Make a pickaxe, armor, and weapons...then enchant them.

Circle the correct **plural noun** for each picture.

helmet	helmset	helmetes	helmets
sword	sworde	swords	swordesrs
block	blox	blockes	blocks
bone	bones	bons	boneses
pickaxe	pickaxis	pickaxes	pickaxese
wolf	wolves	wolfes	wolfs

What do you say to an iron creature that keeps interrupting you?
"Golem away, I'm busy!"

Draw a line to connect each **singular** word with its **plural** form.

boot	zombies
shield	axes
book	horses
arrow	books
horse	boots
zombie	arrows
axe	shields

MINECRAFT MISSION

Enchanted weapons will come in handy on your adventure and are also part of this mission.

This *outside* of this book mission is a game to make and play with a friend.

You'll need:

- 28 index cards
- A pencil

Make the game:

- Write a word on each card.

Use these words:		queen	wolf	dig
dog	ice	plank	vine	block
cat	helmet	mob	under	axe
bees	gold	laugh	tool	yellow
armor	fish	king	stop	ore
nest	egg	jump	run	zombie

- Shuffle the cards and give five to each player.

How to play:

- Pick one card. Say the word and its first letter.

- If a player has a word that starts with the next letter in the alphabet, they must give that card to you. You keep going and call out a word from another card.

- If no one has a word that starts with the next letter, draw a new card. Then it's the next player's turn.

- The first person to have ten cards wins the game!

MINECRAFT

ENCHANT

Great job! You earned a badge! Place your sticker here.

MINECRAFT
REPAIR

PORTAL PROJECT

You've found a gap between some trees. It's the entrance to a new forest!

In this adventure, you will....

Locate a Nether portal.

Break obsidian.

Repair a ruined portal.

Craft flint and steel.

Let's get started!

As you explore the forest, winding your way through the trees, you spot something far in the distance. It's a ruined Nether portal!

Sharpen your addition skills and solve each problem.

23 + 16 = 39   55 + 12 = ___

15 + 33 = ___   41 + 39 = ___

20 + 60 = ___   34 + 16 = ___

70 + 18 = ___

67 + 23 = ___

Follow the rules in the box below to color and complete the picture.

Use these rules:
10 = orange   30 = blue   70 = green   90 = yellow
20 = red   50 = brown   80 = white   100 = purple

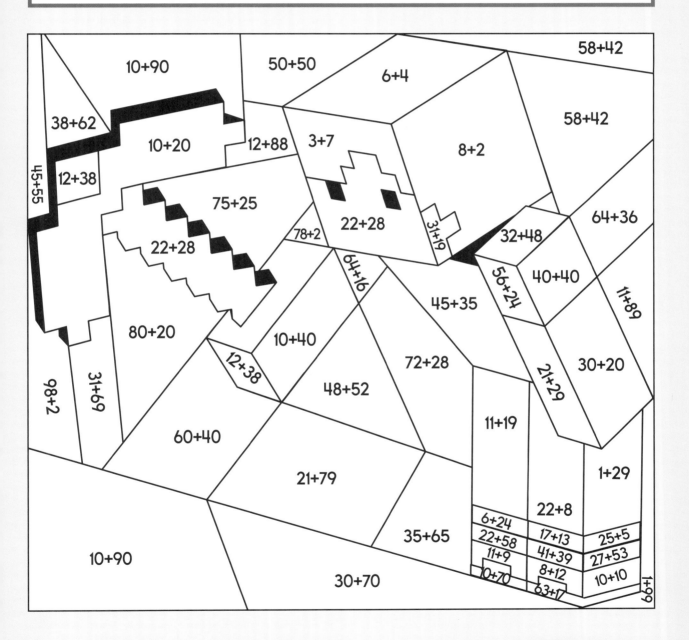

You'll need obsidian to repair that portal. Locate and then mine some with your diamond pickaxe.

Cross out one piece of obsidian in each problem to leave the correct answer. The first one has been done for you.

30 - 20 = 1 ~~8~~ 0

99 - 19 = 8 0 9

22 - 11 = 1 2 1

69 - 23 = 4 6 9

78 - 21 = 2 5 7

65 - 14 = 5 1 2

MINECRAFT FACT: Crying obsidian is not usable in a portal and can only be harvested with a diamond or netherite pickaxe.

Read each word problem. Then rewrite it as a math problem and solve.

I found 45 pieces of obsidian.
I broke 12 of them.

How many pieces of obsidian are left?

$$\begin{array}{r} \underline{} \\ -\underline{} \\ \underline{} \end{array}$$

I saw a portal 55 steps away.
I took 20 steps toward it.

How many steps away is the portal now?

$$\begin{array}{r} \underline{} \\ -\underline{} \\ \underline{} \end{array}$$

35 skeletons were chasing me.
11 of them burned in the sun.

How many skeletons are still following me?

$$\begin{array}{r} \underline{} \\ -\underline{} \\ \underline{} \end{array}$$

68 mobs were near the portal.
I defeated 46 of them.

How many enemies do I still have to fight?

$$\begin{array}{r} \underline{} \\ -\underline{} \\ \underline{} \end{array}$$

You carry your obsidian through the forest. You have to pass many hills and trees to reach the portal.

Read each word problem. Then use the spaces on the right to help find the difference when you subtract. The first one has been done for you.

I saw 93 trees. I passed 17 of them. **How many were ahead of me?**

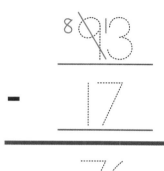

$$
\begin{array}{r}
{}^{8}\cancel{9}3 \\
-\ 17 \\
\hline
76
\end{array}
$$

I turned left along a row of 82 trees. I passed 73 of them. **How many were left?**

$$
\begin{array}{r}
\underline{} \\
-\ \underline{} \\
\hline
\underline{}
\end{array}
$$

I reached a line of 40 trees. I passed 19 of them. **How many were left?**

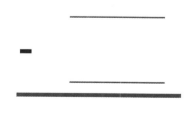

$$
\begin{array}{r}
\underline{} \\
-\ \underline{} \\
\hline
\underline{}
\end{array}
$$

MINECRAFT FACT: To get a ruined Nether portal working again, you will have to fill gaps in the frame and replace any crying obsidian with ordinary obsidian.

I turned right and saw 43 trees in my way. I passed 14 of them.

How many were still there?

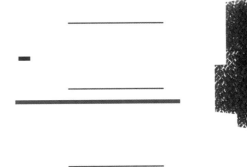

$$-\ \underline{\qquad}$$
$$\underline{\qquad}$$

I ran quickly around a corner, and there were 22 trees in my way. I walked around 13 of them.

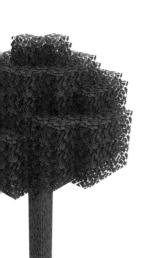

How many were still in the way?

$$-\ \underline{\qquad}$$
$$\underline{\qquad}$$

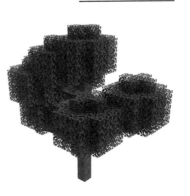

Copy each answer in order into the spaces below. Then solve the problem. It will tell you how much obsidian it will take to patch the portal.

$$76 - \underline{\qquad} - \underline{\qquad} - \underline{\qquad} - \underline{\qquad} = \underline{\qquad}$$

You did it! Place your sticker here.

Dig in the gravel to mine flint. Then you can combine it with iron to craft flint and steel.

Write how many of each item are in each group and add them together. Then write the multiplication equation that means the same thing. The first one has been done for you.

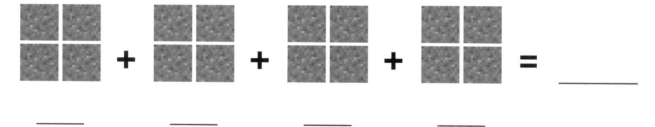

$$3 + 3 + 3 + 3 = 12$$

$$3 \times 4 = 12$$

$$\underline{} + \underline{} + \underline{} + \underline{} = \underline{}$$

$$\underline{} \times \underline{} = \underline{}$$

$$\underline{} + \underline{} + \underline{} + \underline{} + \underline{} = \underline{}$$

$$\underline{} \times \underline{} = \underline{}$$

Where did the mobs buy their portal? A spawn shop.

_____ + _____ + _____ = _____

| ×   = |
| ___ ___ _____ |

_____ + _____ + _____ + _____ = _____

| ×   = |
| ___ ___ _____ |

_____ + _____ + _____ = _____

| ×   = |
| ___ ___ _____ |

You can use your flint and steel to activate the Nether portal. Before you enter, complete this challenge.

This mission sends you on a search *inside* this book. There are items hidden in the top borders of most pages!

Search for pages that have **flint and steel** ( ) hidden at the top. Add the numbers for that page, then write each total in a square of the portal below.

Finally, add the numbers in all the squares and write that number in the center of the portal.

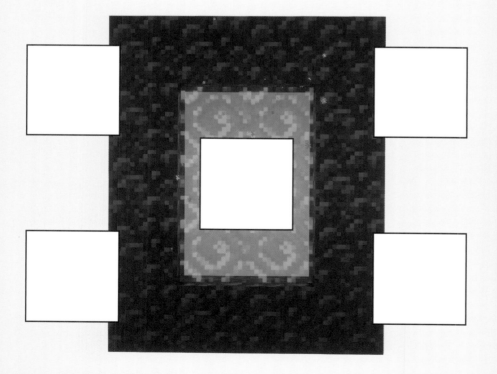

Great job! You earned a badge! Place your sticker here.

WELCOME TO THE NETHER

You stepped through the portal and reached an unfamiliar realm!

In this adventure, you will....

Craft a gold helmet.

Discover new biomes.

Find a bastion.

Barter with piglins.

Let's get started!

WORDS WITH SILENT E

Piglins love gold! Craft a gold helmet to attract their attention.

Look at the words next to each gold item. Many of them can become new words by adding a **silent e** to the end.

Complete only the words that become a new word with a **silent e** ending.

pin__   bug__   fin__

not__   gum__   pig__

hop__   star__   car__

sun__   dig__   bit__

Write four more words that have a **silent e**.

_____   _____

_____   _____

MINECRAFT FACT: Gold armor will keep piglins from attacking you.

Find all the **silent e** words in this word search. Words go up, down, across, backward, and diagonally. When you're finished, the leftover letters will tell you something you see in the distance.

Find these words:

ape	bike	dine	move	some	vine
ate	bite	hide	name	take	wake
beware	come	joke	note	tile	

```
B  E  W  A  R  E  K  O  J
A  T  A  K  E  P  A  E  B
C  B  K  A  E  L  I  T  I
E  O  E  E  S  T  E  O  K
T  E  M  A  N  V  I  N  E
I  A  T  E  O  I  I  O  N
B  S  O  M  E  E  D  I  H
```

___ ___ ___ ___ ___ ___ ___ ___

To reach the bastion, you'll have to travel through many new and strange places.

Using the provided letter blends, complete all of the words in each Nether biome.

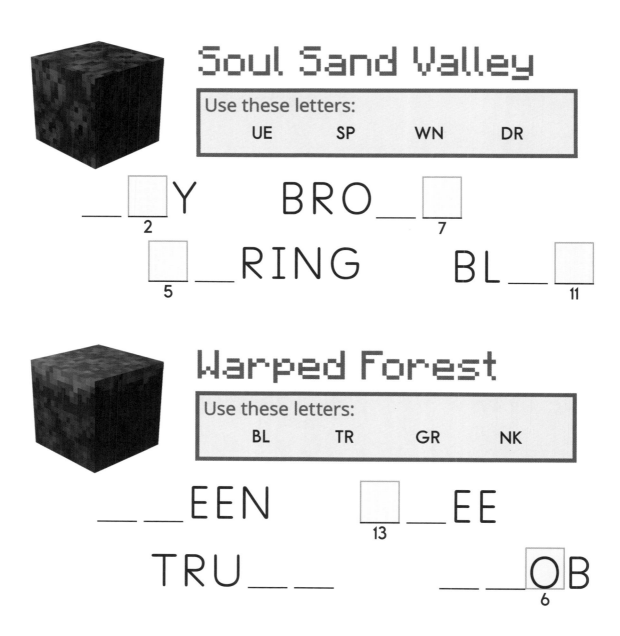

Soul Sand Valley

Use these letters:

UE   SP   WN   DR

___☐Y   BRO___☐
   2   7

☐___RING   BL___☐
 5   11

Warped Forest

Use these letters:

BL   TR   GR   NK

___ ___EEN   ☐___EE
                13

TRU___ ___   ___ ___OB
                      6

Basalt Deltas

Use these letters:

CK   SP   RK   ST

DA___   ___IKE
                     3

☐ __ONE   BLA__☐
12   9   9

Nether Wastes

Use these letters:

RT   SH   CK   FL

RO☐__   ☐__AMES
    1   8

MU___ROOM   FO☐__
        9   4   10

Write the letters from each shaded space above into the space below with the matching number to spell where you'll go next.

__ __ __ __ __ __ __   __ __ __ __ __ __
1   2   3   4   5   6   7   8   9 10 11 12 13

You did it! Place your sticker here.

You've reached a crimson forest. A dark structure looms in the distance. It's the bastion!

Sort the words from the list below into categories by writing them in the correct lists and matching the number of letters to the spaces provided. Cross each word out as you categorize it. The leftover words will tell you what's going to happen next.

axe   piglins   blaze   carrot   gold   hoe   ghast

iron   zombie   shovel   diamond   stew   skeleton   will

beetroot   barter   pickaxe   leather   with   you   apple

Hostile Mobs

_ _ _ _ _

_ _ _ _ _ _

_ _ _ _ _

_ _ _ _ _ _ _

MINECRAFT FACT: Piglins are all around the Nether, but they gather in large numbers around bastion remnants.

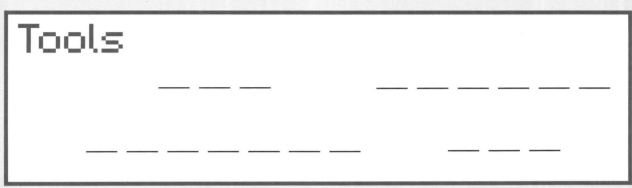

Tools

__ __ __　__ __ __ __ __

__ __ __ __ __ __ __　__ __ __

Materials

__ __ __ __ __ __ __

__ __ __ __ __ __ __

__ __ __　__ __ __ __

Food

__ __ __ __ __ __

__ __ __ __ __

__ __ __ __ __ __ __ __

__ __ __ __

__ __ __ __ __ __ __　__ __ __ __

__ __ __ __ __　__ __ __ __　__ __ __

The bastion is full of piglins. Throw something at their feet, and they will barter with you.

Trace a line from each word to its **antonym** (word that means the opposite).

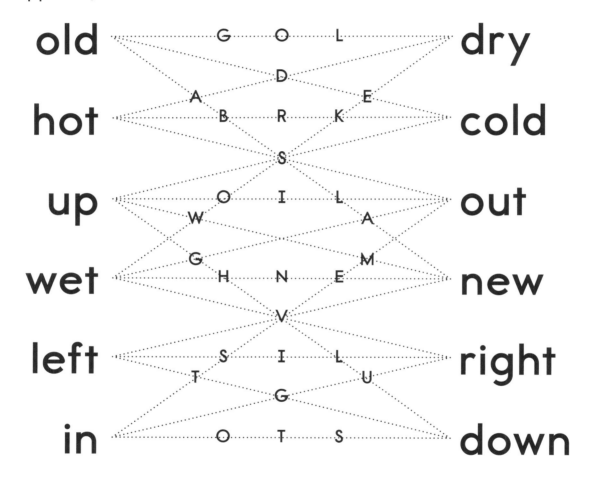

old   G O L   dry
            D
         A   E
hot   B R K   cold
            S
up   O I L   out
      W   A
      G   M
wet   H N E   new
            V
left S I L   right
     T   U
         G
in   O T S   down

Now copy the letters that remain into the spaces below. They will spell what you should throw to the piglins.

___ ___ ___ ___   ___ ___ ___ ___ ___ ___

What collects in a mob's pockets? *Pig-LINT.*

Trace a line from each word to its **synonym** (word that means the same thing).

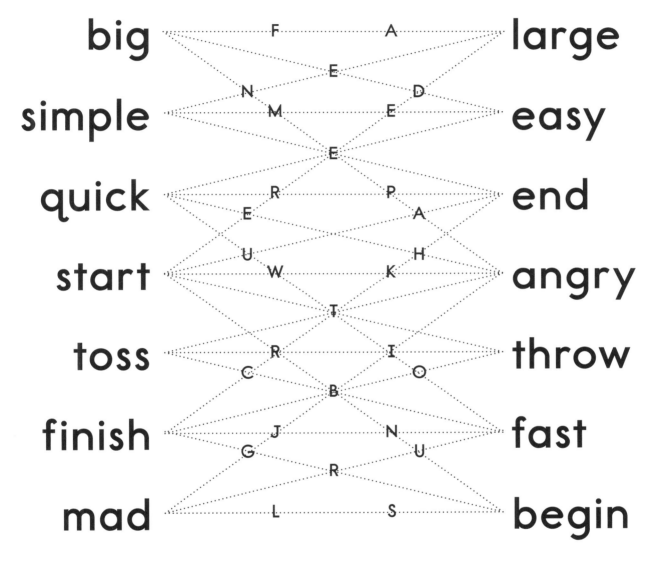

big   large

simple   easy

quick   end

start   angry

toss   throw

finish   fast

mad   begin

Now copy the letters that remain into the spaces below. They will spell what the piglins gave you.

___ ___ ___ ___ ___ ___   ___ ___ ___ ___ ___ ___

Before you head deeper into the Nether, take a break and try this challenge.

This is another mission that takes you *outside* of this book: a rhyming quest! How many matching words that rhyme can you find in your world?

For each Minecraft word in the list below, search for something in or around your house that rhymes with it. Write the rhyming word next to each one on the list when you find it to keep track.

rock _____

boat _____

tree _____

block _____

mine _____

Once you're done, celebrate with a sticker on this page!

Great job! You earned a badge! Place your sticker here.

MINE

IT'S NOW OR NETHER

Deeper into the Nether, you can mine, craft, and upgrade.

In this adventure, you will....

Dig deep.

Find ancient debris.

Smelt ore.

Craft netherite ingots.

Let's get started!

Dig deep into the ground, and you'll find something very special.

Find all the pairs of matching shapes, then color them.

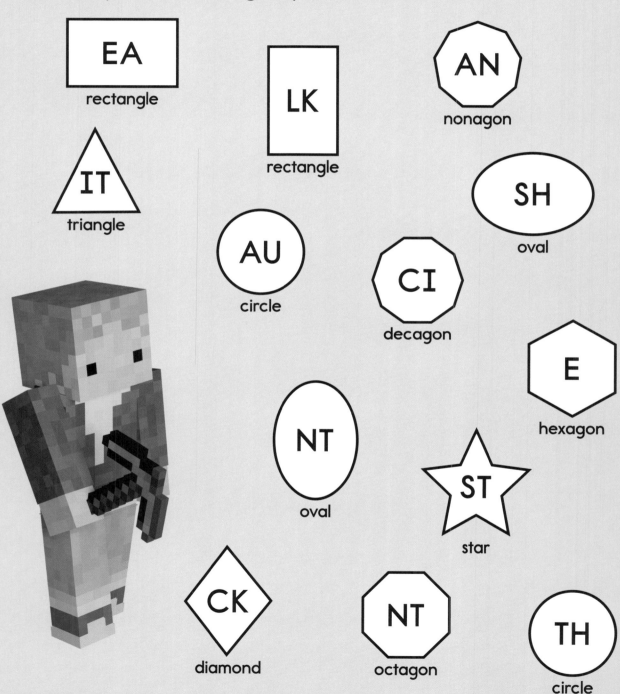

EA
rectangle

LK
rectangle

AN
nonagon

IT
triangle

SH
oval

AU
circle

CI
decagon

E
hexagon

NT
oval

ST
star

CK
diamond

NT
octagon

TH
circle

**MINECRAFT FACT: Netherrack is a stone block
that can be found all over the Nether.**

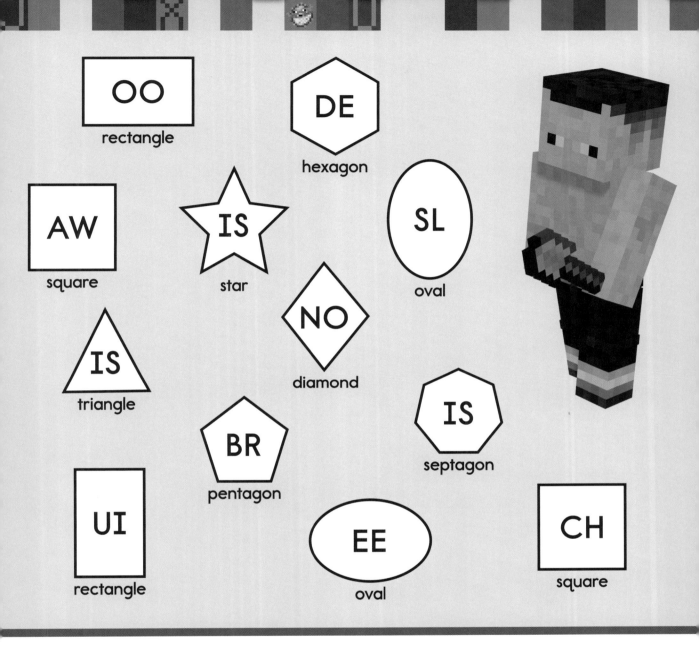

OO
rectangle

DE
hexagon

SL
oval

AW
square

IS
star

IS
triangle

NO
diamond

IS
septagon

BR
pentagon

UI
rectangle

EE
oval

CH
square

Copy the letters from the leftover shapes into the spaces below.
They'll spell what you've found.

_ _ _ _ _ _ _ _ _ _ _ _

Keep digging, but be careful! The Nether is full of lava, so move forward with caution.

Follow the tunnels from **START** to **END**. You'll find many **cubes** (⬓), **spheres** (◯), **cones** (◁), and **cylinders** (⬭). You cannot move from one shape to another of the same shape, and you cannot cross lava!

Keep track of the **ancient debris** (▣) you pass along the way. Each time you pass a block of ancient debris, fill in one block. If you can collect at least ten blocks of ancient debris, you're a winner!

ATTEMPT 1:

ATTEMPT 2:

ATTEMPT 3:

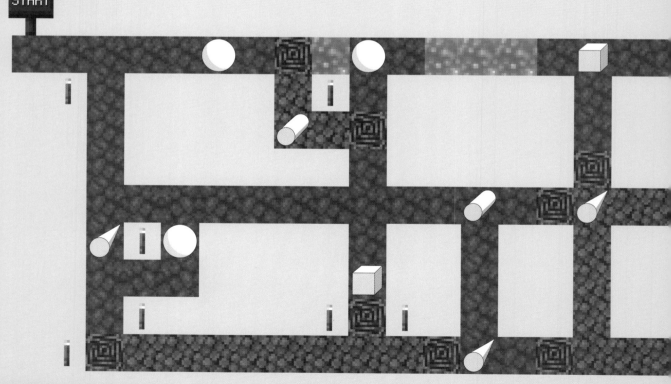

MINECRAFT FACT: Ancient debris is super rare and hidden under the netherrack floor.

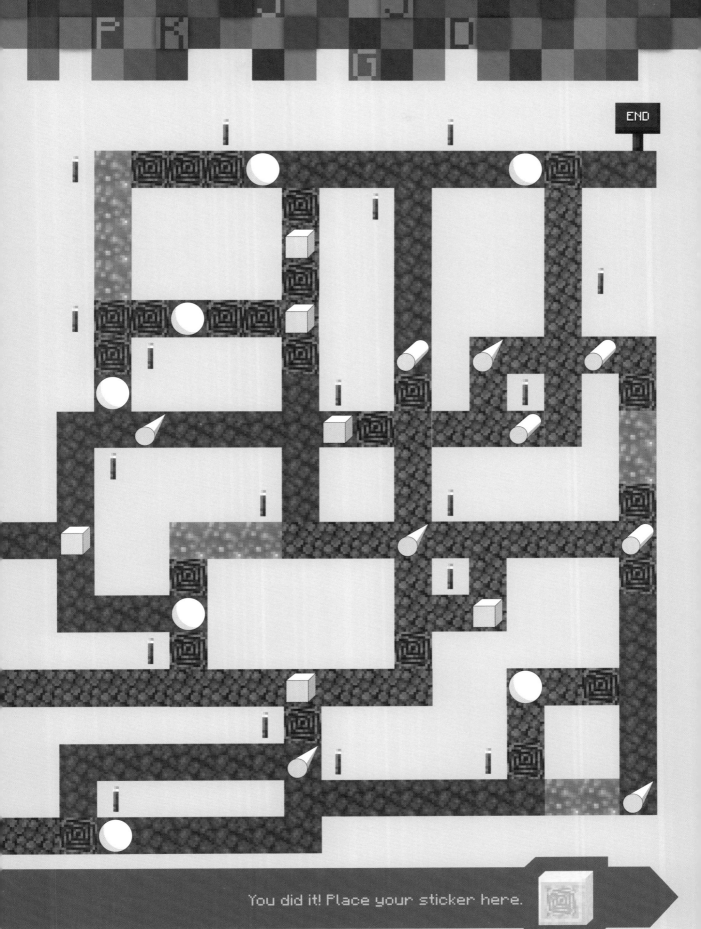

END

You did it! Place your sticker here.

Fire up your furnace to smelt the ancient debris into netherite scraps.

Count the number of ancient debris blocks in each group. Then color the row in the chart on page 79 that matches the amount.

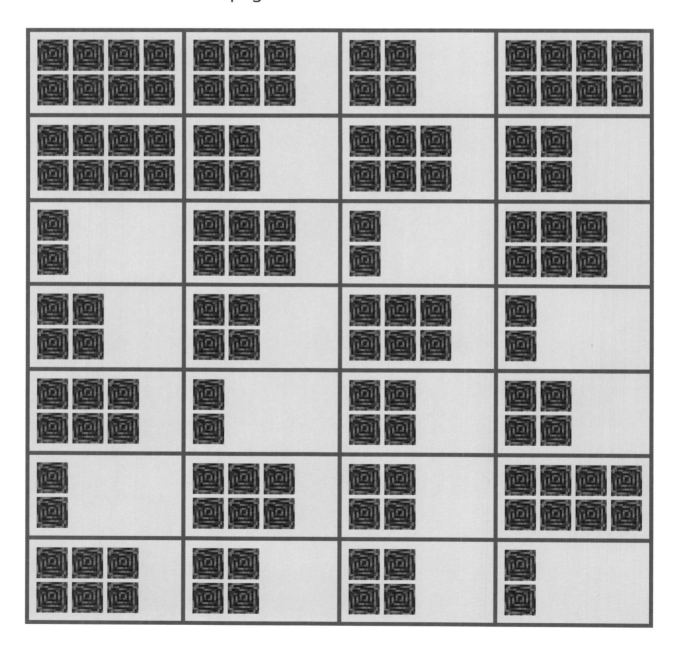

MINECRAFT FACT: Ancient debris can float on lava and is immune to burning.

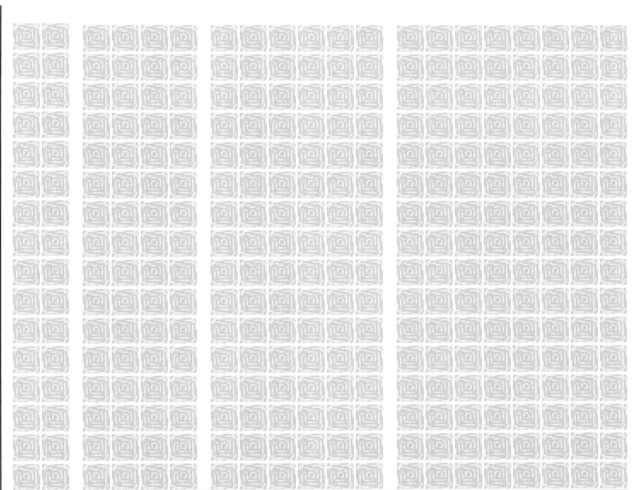

groups of 2	groups of 4	groups of 6	groups of 8

How many groups have two pieces? _____

How many have four pieces? _____

How many have six pieces? _____

How many have eight pieces? _____

With some gold ingots, you can craft netherite scraps into netherite ingots.

Trace an **X** in the chart below for every object you see.

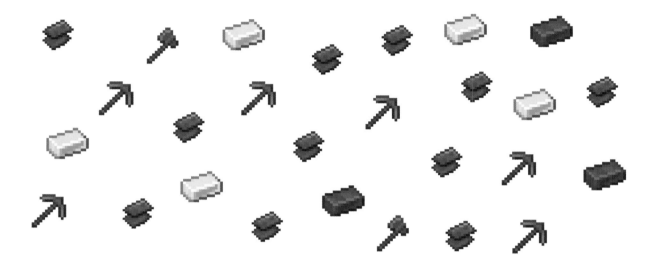

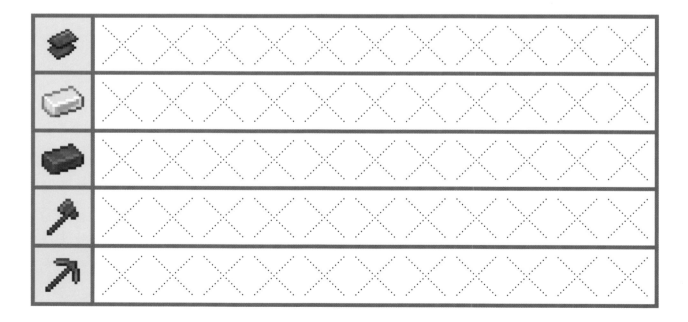

Why did the adventurers wear netherite? They were invited to a block party!

Now fill in this graph. Color one square for every **X** you drew on page 80.

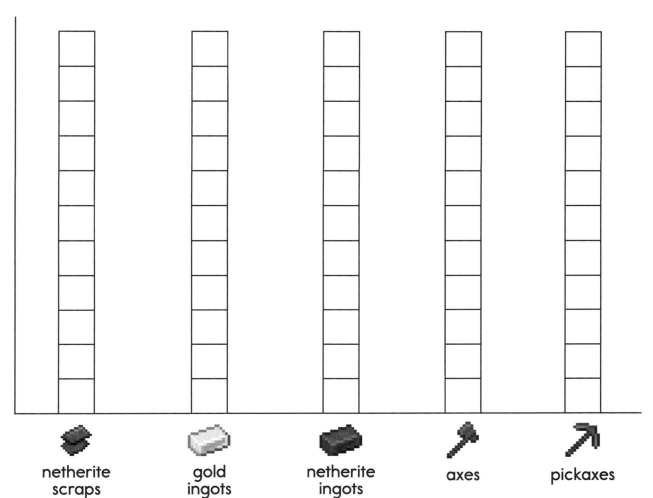

How many **pickaxes** (⛏) are there? _____

Which item has the **fewest** squares? _____

Which item has the **most** squares? _____

How many more **scraps** (⬛) than **gold ingots** (◻) are there? _____

MINECRAFT MISSION

With netherite ingots, you can upgrade useful diamond items. Take this challenge to get ready for a final battle.

This mission sends you on a search *inside* this book. There are items hidden in the top borders of most pages!

Search for **netherite ingots** (⬛). Each one will have a letter on it. Copy all the letters from the ingots to the lines below. (Hint: The order doesn't matter.)

____ ____ ____ ____ ____

____ ____ ____ ____ ____

____ ____ ____ ____ ____

Count how many of each letter you found. Write one of each letter below, going in order from the fewest to the most letters.

Then read what you upgraded with your netherite!

___ ___ ___ ___ ___

MINECRAFT

MINE

Great job! You earned a badge! Place your sticker here.

CONQUER

SUIT UP FOR BATTLE

With your new netherite sword, you're ready to take on a fortress.

In this adventure, you will...

Drink a potion.

Dodge fireballs.

Destroy a spawner.

Fight blazes.

Let's get started!

You're going to battle blazes, so it's a good idea to drink a helpful potion first.

Circle every potion that is next to a **noun** (a person, place, or thing).

chest   tower

pink   farm

hot   dig

cave   push

helmet   down

save   house

sword   jump

MINECRAFT FACT: Potions of Fire Resistance can be obtained from piglins and will help protect you from blaze attacks.

Circle the **nouns** in each column. Trace the lines from each noun on the left to those that connect on the right.

When you're done, write the words in the middle that are not crossed out to see how the potion helps you.

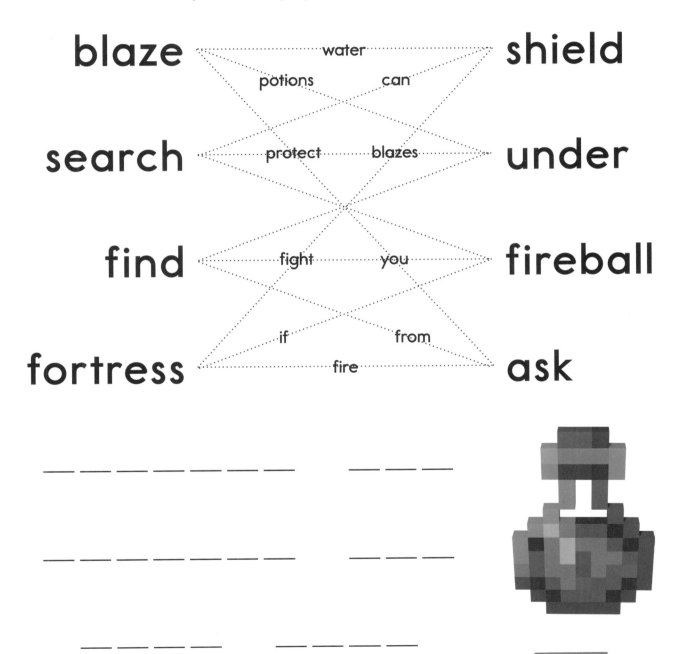

blaze   water   shield

        potions   can

search   protect   blazes   under

find   fight   you   fireball

        if   from

fortress   fire   ask

_ _ _ _ _ _ _   _ _ _ _ _

_ _ _ _ _ _ _   _ _ _ _

_ _ _ _   _ _ _ _

Here come the fireballs. Watch out!

Read each pair of words and circle the one that is a **verb** (an action word or thing that you can do).

Then count the number of letters in the verb and underline the word next to the fireball with that number.

eat	tree

grow	sunshine

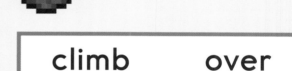

climb	over

build	portal

job	make

silver	hold

fix	lake

bake	yellow

MINECRAFT FACT: Netherite items are resistant to fire and lava.

⑧ near	③ that	⑥ fish
④ was	⑤ a	⑦ want
⑤ close	④ call	② intense
② them	⑦ will	④ but
③ you	④ survived	⑥ swam

Write the words you underlined into the spaces below.
When you're done, read what happened!

___ ___ ___ ___   ___ ___ ___   ___

___ ___ ___ ___ ___   ___ ___ ___ ___   ___ ___ ___

___ ___ ___   ___ ___ ___ ___ ___ ___ ___

These blazes will keep attacking until you take action!

Cross out all the words that are *not* **adjectives** (words that describe).

run

big

burn

ready

potion

tomato

family

excellent

angry

gather

kind

fight

tiny

win

huge

equal

sloppy

MINECRAFT FACT: Breaking the blazes' spawner will stop more blazes from appearing.

you

use

hide

egg

pink

sword

creeper

alarmed

wet

armor

new

eager

red

Copy the first letter of each remaining word into the spaces below. This will tell you how to stop the blazes.

_ _ _ _ _ _ _ _ _

_ _ _ _ _ _ _

You did it! Place your sticker here.

This is it! No new blazes are spawning, but you still need to battle the existing blazes.

Follow the arrow and move as many spaces in that direction as there are letters in the word. When you stop at a new space, write that word on page 91. Keep going until you reach the yellow space at the bottom right. The first two words have been done for you.

It ↓	saw →	all ↓	fire ←	blazes ↓	I →	beat ←	walk ↓
piglin →	not ↓	lava ↓	lose →	did ←	I ←	arrow ←	blast ↓
was ↓	battle →	sheep →	ran ↓	went ←	am →	gone ↓	dragon ←
apple →	dig ↓	of →	cow ↓	the ↑	but ↑	mobs ←	bow ↑
zombie →	think →	to ↓	then ↑	dark ←	if ↓	I ↓	he ↓
a ↓	make →	we ↑	shine ↑	what ←	it ↑	would ←	tower ↑
tough →	seeds ↑	afraid ↑	she ←	and →	fight ↑	battle ←	won

I† was _ _ _ _ _ _

_ _ _ _ _ .   _   _ _ _

_ _   _ _ _ _ _   _

_ _ _ _ _   _ _ _ _   _ _ ,

_ _ _   _ _   _ _ _ _

_ _ _   _ _   _ _ _

_ _ _ _ _ _   _ _ _   _ _ _ !

Now read all the words you wrote to find out what you've done.

MINECRAFT MISSION

You defeated the blazes. You're a hero in Minecraft... and beyond!

You've discovered so many things within these pages! Now try one last mission *outside* this book and search for things in the real world.

Below is a list of ten things to find on an ultimate scavenger hunt. Look in places like your kitchen or living room. You can search outside, too!

Check off the items as you find them. If you can find four of these things...not bad. Keep going. If you can find six things, you're an excellent explorer. Find everything on this list, and you're a Minecraft Mission Superstar!

Super Scavenger Hunt:

• A shovel

• Something with **hexagons** on it

• The word **friend** on a page in a book (not this book!)

• Something that ends with **ell**

• Something with many **odd** numbers on it but no **even** numbers

• Two things that end in a **silent e**

• Any three things that **rhyme**

MINECRAFT

CONQUER

ANSWERS

Pages 4–5
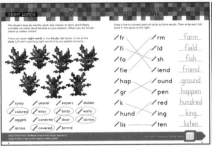

Pages 6–7
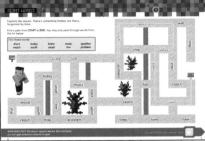

Pages 8–9
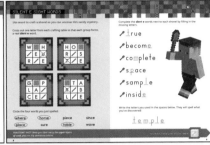

Pages 10–11

Pages 14–15
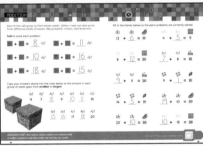

Pages 16–17
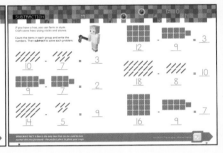

Pages 18–19
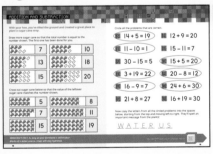

Pages 20–21
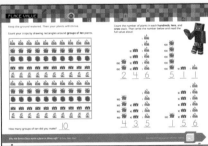

Page 22

Pages 26–27

Pages 28–29
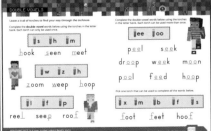

Pages 30–31
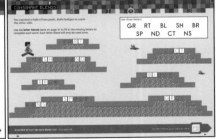

Pages 34–35

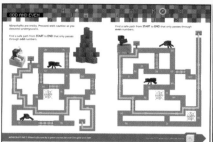

Pages 36–37

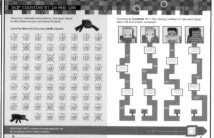

Pages 38–39

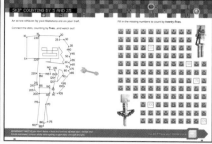

Pages 40–41

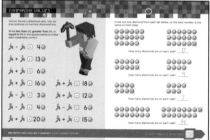

Page 42

Page 46

Pages 48–49

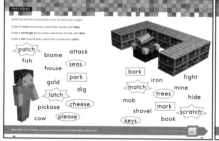

Pages 50–51

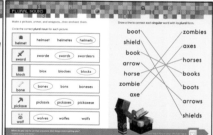

Pages 54–55

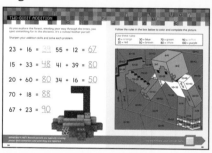

Pages 56–57

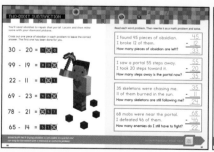

Pages 58–59

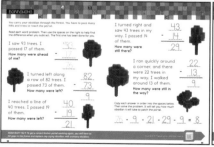

Pages 60–61

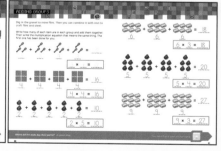

Page 62

Pages 64–65

Pages 66–67

Pages 68–69

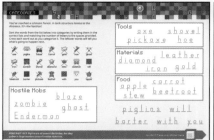

CATEGORIES

Tools: axe, shovel, pickaxe, hoe

Materials: diamond, leather, iron, gold

Food: apple, carrot, stew, beetroot

Hostile Mobs: zombie, blaze, Enderman, ghast

piglins will barter with you

Pages 70–71

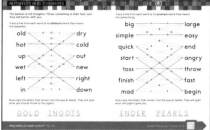

ANTONYMS AND SYNONYMS

old – dry / hot – cold / up – out / wet – new / left – right / in – down

big – large / simple – easy / quick – end / start – angry / toss – throw / finish – fast / mad – begin

GOLD INGOTS

ENDER PEARLS

Pages 74–75

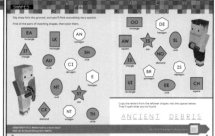

SHAPES

ANCIENT DEBRIS

Pages 78–79

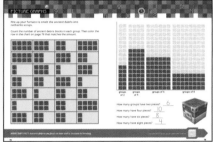

PICTURE GRAPHS

How many groups have two pieces? 6
How many have four pieces? 10
How many have six pieces? 8
How many have eight pieces? 4

Pages 80–81

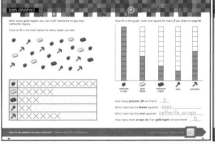

BAR GRAPHS

How many pickaxes are there? 6
Which item has the fewest squares? axes
Which item has the most squares? netherite scraps
How many more scraps than gold ingots are there? 6

Page 82

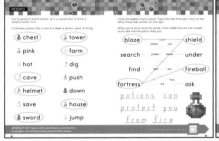

MINECRAFT MISSION

D R R D R
D O D W O
D S R O W

SWORD

Pages 84–85

NOUNS

chest, pink, hot, cave, helmet, save, sword, tower, farm, dig, push, down, house, jump

potions can protect you from fire

Pages 86–87

VERBS

near, that, fish, was, a, want, close, call, intense, them, will, but, you, survived, swam

eat, tree, grow, sunshine, climb, over, build, portal, job, make, silver, hold, fix, lake, bake, yellow

that was a close call but you survived

Pages 88–89

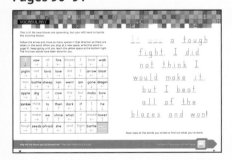

ADJECTIVES

break the spawner

Pages 90–91

VOCABULARY

It was a tough fight. I did not think I would make it, but I beat all of the blazes and won!

MINECRAFT ACHIEVEMENT

Let it be known
throughout the Nether:

_____
YOUR NAME

has completed an
adventure filled with
MINECRAFT MISSIONS!

GRADE 2

MINECRAFT MINECRAFT

MINECRAFT CONQUER

MINECRAFT MINE

MINECRAFT BARTER

MINECRAFT REPAIR

MINECRAFT ENCHANT

MINECRAFT DISCOVER

MINECRAFT GROW

MINECRAFT EXPLORE

MINECRAFT SEARCH